Smoke and Roses

Assia,

Where do I even begin? Well, I would like to thank you from the bottom of my soul for supporting me and my art the minute I met you. Thank you for always giving me feedback and showing me love. Hearing your art has played a huge role, and has inspired, in the creation of my poems. So, please do the world a favour, and never stop writing. You are a force. Sending you love with all my heart. Can't wait for your book.

xo, adel aida

*Smoke
and
Roses*

Adelaide Clare Attard

Life Rattle Press   Toronto, Canada

Smoke and Roses

Published by Life Rattle New Writers Series
Life Rattle
Toronto, Ontario

Stories copyright © 2017 by Adelaide Clare Attard

All rights reserved. The use of any parts of publication reproduced, transmitted in any form or by any means, electronic, mechanical, photocopying, recording or otherwise, or stored in a retrieval system, without prior consent of the author is an infringement on the copyright law.

ISBN 978-1-987936-29-2

Cover design by Jack Jozwik
Copy edited by Lyndsay Sinko
Typeset and design by Adelaide Clare Attard and Jack Jozwik
Rose illustration in *About the Author* by Jodie Aquino

To Mom, Dad, Lexi, Nannu and Jack,
the loves of my life.

"Ash on an old man's sleeve
is all the ash burnt roses leave."

-T.S. Eliot, *The Little Gidding*

Contents

The Daughter
The Rose. *13*
The Broken Box. *21*

The Child
Leonard. *31*
Playing Cards *37*
Shampoo. *43*

The Traveller
Of Giving and Goodbyes *51*
Joy *61*
Esther *67*
Houston's *75*

The Woman
Selfish *83*
0.1% *89*
All the Good Bits. *97*
Just Like Your Mother. *103*
Appendix *109*

The Poet *118-136*

The Daughter

The Rose

"Karen, can you stop for a second? I'm getting lightheaded." I groan.

I rest my head on the black leather tattoo chair. Chronic Ink Tattoo's glass doors open and close as customers come and go.

"Lightheaded? Do you need a glass of water? Let's take a five minute break," Karen says through her thick Japanese accent. She sits on a round stool with wheels. Her jean Bermuda shorts collect around her thin waist.

My boyfriend Jack hands me my marble S'Well water bottle.

He puts his warm palm on my warm forehead.

"You okay?"

"Yeah, my body's just in shock, I guess. No regrets, though. This is the best birthday present I've ever given myself." I laugh.

"Well, it looks really good!"

Jack's brown curly hair grazes my leg, as he gets closer to the tattoo.

I take a deep breath and tell Karen to resume. She tears herself away from her Samsung phone and places it face down on the computer desk. Karen snaps on a new pair of blue latex gloves. She picks up the tattoo gun from a metal surgical table covered in inkpots, tubs of Vaseline and tiny plastic bags filled with needles.

"Ready?"

"Yeah." I inhale and smile.

I close my eyes and pretend the buzzing is normal. Karen stops.

"Hey, how do you feel about thorns?"

I look at my unfinished rose tattoo. My inner left calf is a fog of blue faded pen and smudged black ink. Japanese dubstep muffles in the background.

"Well, it *is* a rose, so I guess it needs thorns. Go for it," I say.

~~~

"*Pupa*, wait a second, I have to cut these off before you can hold it!"

I stand beside the outdoor air conditioning unit in Nannu's big garden behind his house in Mississauga. I raise my hand over my brows to block the sun. My multicoloured Birkenstocks disappear in the trimmed grass. Roses of red, orange and yellow sway in the May wind and hide behind tiny green leaves. Some sag, some stand straight.

I like the yellow one.

The outer petals begin to brown, but the petals in the middle are ready to bloom. This rose is the colour of the song that me and Daddy love: Yellow by Coldplay. The petals need some love. I can love them.

My small hand lets go of the yellow rose Nannu snipped off the bush for me. His large, calloused fingers pluck it from my palm. Nannu lifts a pair of hedge clippers from the grass and snips off all the thorns from the rose.

"Why you chose the yellow one and not the red, *Pupa*?" Pupa means doll in Maltese. According to Nannu, I looked like a doll when I was a baby.

"Because it's my favourite colour, Nannu!"

He hands back the flower, now without thorns. I smell the blooming rose. It smells like the soft spring breeze.

"Your favourite colour is yellow? You know how to say yellow in Maltese?"

"No." I smile at him.

"Say it with me," he leans next to me and points to my rose. "Say like this, *isfar*." His thick accent surfaces.

"*If-zar*," I try.

"No, *Pupa*, *issss-far*," he corrects me.

"*Issss-far*," I repeat. "Nannu, how do you say rose in Maltese?"

"A rose in Maltese is *fjura*." He runs his rough hands through his silver hair.

I hold the rose up to Nannu's nose. "*Fjura isfar*!"

He laughs and lifts me onto his hip. "That's my *Pupa*! Let's show Nanna."

My pink-checkered shorts bunch around my thighs.

Nannu grasps me in his strong arms. I tug on the collar of his purple polo that says *Glaxo* on it. Nannu says *Glaxo* is the factory Nanna used to work at. He has all kinds of shirts with company's names on them, the kind you get for free.

We pass the row of fruit trees along the wooden fence. The trees stand like soldiers at attention and grow from a bed of deep green grass. A black plastic owl with beady yellow eyes sways back and forth from the highest branch in the green apple tree. Nannu says it's to scare away birds and squirrels from eating the fruits.

I wriggle out of his arms and run through the front door

of Nanna and Nannu's house. As I swing the door open, the smell of warm minestra soup fills my nose. Nanna stands at 5 feet, clad in a well-loved blue apron. Her favourite. She chops veggies on a worn wooden cutting board.

"Nanna, *fjura isfar*!" I stand on my tiptoes and hold the rose up to her face. The petals stroke the lens of her rectangular glasses.

Nanna laughs. Her round body shakes.

"*Fjura isfar*!" Nanna laughs. "Did Nannu teach you that?"

"Yeah, and he even picked this *fjura* for me from the garden!"

She pushes my honey-coloured bangs back with a soft, wrinkled hand. Her gold wedding rings graze my forehead.

"*Pupa*, you need to put the *fjura* in water, or it will die."

She stands on her tip toes, opens the cupboard and grabs a tall drinking glass from the top shelf.

"Take this and fill it up with *ilma*." She hands me the glass.

I walk over to the kitchen sink, stand on my tippy toes and reach for the tap. *Ilma* fills the glass covered in my smudged fingerprints. I pick my rose up off the counter and gently submerge its stem in the water. The stem looks bigger when I put it in *ilma*. I grasp the glass with both hands, watch my feet with each slow step, and place the rose on top of the fruit patterned tablecloth. It rests on the center of the table.

"Look, Nanna and Nannu, I made a decoration!"

"When your Daddy comes to pick you up, you have to show him."

~~~

After dinner, I hear the door click and squeak open.

Nanna's head perks up from washing dishes. "Look who it is!"

The sun sets behind a silhouette of a baldheaded man in a

suit. He closes the door behind him.

"Daddy! Daddy!" I bolt from my spot at the table to the doorway. I wrap my body around his legs.

"Look what I got from Nannu's garden!" I tug his pant leg.

"Addy, can I take my shoes off first?" Dad laughs.

He walks over to the kitchen table. Nanna stands behind him.

"Tell him what it is," Nanna urges.

"*Fjura isfar*!"

Dad laughs, "Another few days at Nanna's and you'll be fluent in Maltese before you start first grade!"

Nannu comes up from the den and into the kitchen.

"Ah-lex, did you see *Pupa's* new find from the garden?"

"Yes, now she can add it to her collection."

~~~

Karen rubs the excess ink off my calf with a wet paper towel. She waves her blue-gloved hand over the tattoo.

"Okay, done. What do you think?" She readjusts her maroon baseball hat, and tucks her short black hair underneath it.

"I love it! Thank you, Karen!" I slide my sweaty body down the black tattoo chair and wrap my arms around her.

"You're welcome." She lets out a nervous laugh.

"What do you think your Nannu is going to say?" Jack asks.

"Hopefully he likes it. He didn't seem to mind the mountain range tattoo on my arm."

"We'll see when we go for Thanksgiving dinner tomorrow."

~~~

I sit on the navy leather couch in Nanna and Nannu's living room with Jack.

"Tell me what he says," Jack whispers, tucking my short, honey hair behind my ear.

I get up from the couch and run to Nannu in the kitchen. I take Nannu's hand and drag him to the doorway of their house filled to the brim with aunts, uncles and cousins. Loud voices fight over other loud voices. The kitchen spills with turkey, potatoes, ravioli and stuffing.

"Nannu, put your shoes on!"

He laughs. "Why *Pupa*?"

"Just do it!"

The front door shuts behind us. In my socks, I run to the backyard, across the lawn, and over to the rosebush by the outdoor air conditioning unit.

"What you taking me here for?"

"I want to show you something, Nannu."

"*Ara* (oh no), what you did?" He laughs, hazel eyes squinting.

I stick out my left leg to reveal a thin rose in black ink. My toes squish into the damp grass.

"You got another one?" He shrieks.

"Yes, but not just for anyone. I got this rose for you. Remember when I was five, and every time I asked for one of these roses, you would get your hedge clippers and cut a rose off for me?" I point to the rosebush.

"Well of course I remember this, even though it was sixteen years ago." He laughs. "*Fjura isfar*, right?"

Deep wrinkles gather around his eyes. He flashes the same crowded smile I've always known.

"Yeah Nannu, *fjura isfar*."

A yellow rose droops off the tired bush that now homes only two *fjuri*. I run into the garage and grab hedge clippers off his tool station.

"Can you cut me this one?" I point at the yellow rose.

He smiles and clips it off the bush. A wrinkled hand gives me the rose.

"Wait, let me cut the thorns off, I don't want you to prick yourself."

The Broken Box

I press my ear up against my wall and listen.

"All of the animals loved her, especially two mice named Gus and Jaq. They'd do anything for the girl they called Cinderelly." I hear Mum's muffled voice in the next room.

For the past two nights, Mum has read my little sister, Lexi, a story.

"Cinderella's stepmother, Lady Tremaine, was cold, cruel, and jealous of Cinderella's charm and beauty. She enjoyed giving Cinderella extra chores to do, such as bathing her cat, Lucifer."

I sit and listen until she stops reading. My bum goes numb.

"The end!" She declares.

I hear the spine of the book crack as Mum closes it.

I sprint from the matted beige carpet and onto my bed. I bury myself underneath the covers.

I force my cough to stay in my throat. I don't want her to know I'm still awake.

"Night, Lulu." Mum closes Lexi's door.

~~~

The next morning, I roll around in bed. My pink tie-dye sheets stick to my back.

I walk to my bathroom and turn on the light. The three lights above the mirror illuminate the lilac colour on the walls. I look at my reflection. My eyes are pink and itchy and I can't breathe through my nose. My bangs stick to my forehead as if I just got out of the shower. My *Beauty and the Beast* nightgown clings to my back. I peer into my room from the hallway and glance at the blaring red numbers that shine from my Lizzie McGuire digital clock.

9:38 AM.

My heart drops.

I run down stairs as my hand skims the smooth, pine banister.

"Hello?" I yell, as I power down the steps.

I get to the bottom step. My heart stops racing and clear snot drips out of both nostrils. Mum sits at the kitchen table and reads the *Toronto Star*. She holds the news in one hand, and a white mug with the Irish flag on it in the other.

Mum looks up over the rims of her purple glasses after sipping from her mug.

"Well don't just stand there! What's all the fuss about?"

I walk over to her. The floor is sticky and crumbs cling to the bottom of my feet.

"Mum, what are you doing here?"

She laughs, "Well this is my house, isn't it?"

I climb on to her lap. Mum's hair is in a messy bun. Auburn strands stick out in every direction. She wears a navy sweater that says "University of Guelph" in yellow capital letters. Her green-checkered pajama bottoms fall past her feet.

The kitchen smells of coffee and toast.

I wipe my nose on my frilly yellow sleeve. "No Mum, I mean, why aren't you at work?"

She puts her purple-rimmed glasses on top of her head, revealing her blue eyes. Usually they look like the sky, but it's raining today.

"Well, sometimes grownups go through times where they can't get a job. It isn't easy to get a good job nowadays. Even Thea's Mum across the street doesn't have one right now."

"Does that mean we are going to be poor?"

She brings the mug up to her mouth and sips. It covers her slender nose. She puts the mug down.

"Not exactly, Ad." She pets my bangs back with her hand. "You see, as long as Daddy works, we will be okay. He can support us for a bit. Married mummies and daddies support each other in any ways that they can."

"I guess. But does this mean you're not going to have a job forever?"

"No, silly girl!" She uses the napkin from her peanut butter toast to blow my nose. Now all I can smell is peanuts.

She crumples it up and puts it on her plate. "This is only temporary. Maybe a few weeks, but Mum's not going to be out of work forever."

I look at her gentle eyes. There are dark circles underneath them. She looks away from me.

Mum pats my bum as a gesture to get off her knee.

"Well, enough adult talk. Let's make the most of this rainy day! Obviously, you're not going to school today. No one wants your stinky germs."

She stands up. The black plastic chair rumbles against the tiled floor as she tucks it in. She leaves the remains of her breakfast on the table and walks down to the basement.

I follow her.

We walk down the unfinished staircase. I step lightly, feeling for any pointy slivers. Mum gets on her tiptoes to reach the light string at the end of the staircase. The naked bulb flickers on. The basement smells of concrete and laundry detergent. Like a cardboard city, boxes of all sizes pile on top of each other.

I reach the last step of the stairs and move onto the cold concrete floor. Mum steps over rolled up posters and my old toys. Old Barbies, Easy Bake oven supplies and dollhouse furniture block her way. She kneels in front of a tower of boxes. Her thin arms struggle to lift the two boxes on top.

"Need help, Mum?"

"No Angel, Mummy's got this." She hugs the first box. Her sweater rises and reveals her pale tummy. Her skin looks like a thin white blanket over a rack of bones.

"Ah, here." She lifts open the cardboard flaps. Mum kneels at a broken box and starts pulling out books. I run over and kneel beside her.

"How about you choose a book? Then we can go upstairs and read!" Mum says as she tucks a loose strand of hair behind her ear.

"Okay, but aren't these books for grown ups?"

She laughs. "Books are stories that take us into different worlds! Now how could that just be for grown ups?"

"I guess."

I wipe my nose on my damp sleeve. I reach my hand into the box of books. These aren't the kinds we have in Mrs. Cameron's grade three class.

"Mum, what's this one? That's a scary cover."

"Oh this? It's called *Dr. Jekyll and Mr. Hyde*. It's a pretty scary story. Dr. Jekyll transforms into Mr. Hyde by using a special potion. It was actually written in 1886, over a hundred years ago!"

I shudder at the image on the front of the book. "The cover is too scary to look at."

The cover has a picture of a man with a top hat on. On his shoulder is a man with a green face and rotting teeth. I place it back into the box.

I dig deeper into the box and pull out the next book I touch. It looks like the name of the book is written in blood. The letters spell D-R-A-C-U-L-A. I sound out the word. *Dra-kyoo-laaaa.*

Mum looks over at me. "I see you've found my favourite book!"

"What's a Dra-kyoo-laaaa?"

"Well, it's a story about a vampire named Count Dracula. He sucks people's blood with his sharp fangs. It takes place in a big castle in Transylvania. A lawyer named Jonathan Harker travels to the castle to help Count Dracula buy a house! Then, spooky stuff happens. Maybe you'd like to read it when you're a bit older."

I ask about the book Mum holds in her hands. There is a picture of a queen dressed in white, and a king dressed in red. A single word pops off the cover: *Mac-beth*.

"Mac-beth?"

"Yes! This is a play written by a man named William Shakespeare. This was written almost four hundred years ago! It's about kings and queens and battles. Three witches tell one of Macbeth's friends, Banquo, that he will one day be the father of boys, who will then be the kings of Scotland. Macbeth doesn't like that, so he sends people to kill his best friend. There's a lot of death and betrayal. There's more, but I won't tell you how it ends."

"Mum! Can you read that to me, please please *please*?"

"Really?" She laughs. "You know I would never say no to reading you something. Let's go upstairs then!"

I dash up the stairs on my hands and feet, sprint down the cold hardwood hallway, run up the stairs to my room and jump into my unmade bed. As I wait for Mum, I look out the window.

The sky is gray and fog covers the tops of houses. The clouds are swollen from rainfall. Puddles on the road start rippling as the rain sprinkles the ground. The tapping of rain hums. My light blue walls become a deeper blue as the clouds huddle together.

Mum finally catches up with me. She holds Macbeth close to her chest. In her other hand is a glass of water and a silver Tylenol Cold Kids package. I can see a single purple pill hiding inside.

"Okay, before I read to you, take this."

She sets the glass and the purple pill on my nightstand, right next to my digital clock. I pick up the pill and chew it.

"Ehk! Yuck!"

"You've gotta take it, Ad."

I scrunch up my face, drink, and swallow.

Mum tucks me under the covers. The rain taps at my window. Mum kneels beside my bed the way she knelt beside the box of books. She smells like Hemp lotion, baby powder and coffee. Mum takes her glasses off the top of her head and puts them on. She pinches the corners of the first few pages, turns them slowly, and studies the book as if she were looking through old pictures.

She clears her throat. "Act one, scene one. A desert place. Thunder and lightning. Enter three witches." She changes her voice to sound like the witches on TV. She scrunches her nose to get in character, "When shall we three meet again? In thunder, lightning, or in rain?"

She changes her voice again to say, "Second witch" and changes back to the Witch Voice, "When the hurlyburly's done, when the battle's lost and won."

"*Third witch*, That will be 'ere the set of sun."

I close my eyes and picture three witches. Each witch looks like the one from Snow White, with a hooked nose, gray hair and a black cloak.

"Double, double toil and trouble; Fire burn and caldron bubble." Mum gestures in a stirring motion and sneaks out a witchy laugh in between the lines.

The rain continues to tap my window.

~~~

Every night of the week, Mum read me Macbeth.
I stopped eavesdropping on Lexi's stories.

The Child

Leonard

It's recess. I sit at the desk closest to the blackboard. Sheets of blank paper lay in front of me. Dull, chipped pencil crayons of different lengths lay in a messy pile around the papers, waiting to be sharpened. I swipe my sharp HB pencil across the blank white page, creating squiggly lines, adding leaves onto some vines.

Ms. Kappl sits at a large rectangular desk right next to the blackboard. Her desk is covered in papers and *Wizard of Oz* figurines. I watch as she marks yesterday's math tests. She swooshes red pen checkmarks on each page and places the tests in a neat pile beside her.

Children's laughter and screaming mixes with the whip of jump ropes on concrete, and hollow booms of nearly deflated basketballs on bricks walls. After every few minutes a high-pitched whistle sounds. That means someone is being sent on "the line." The line is where kids have to stand for the rest of recess if they did something bad. They stand on a long line drawn in mustard yellow paint. The line is chipping now, wearing away each time it rains. After hearing five whistles, I know there are five kids standing on the line.

I take a break from colouring my grape vines, too lazy

to sharpen the violet Crayola pencil crayon. I push my chair back, step away from my desk and walk over to the window. My light-up *Dora the Explorer* shoes blink with each step I make.

"So Long Marianne" plays from a chunky silver stereo, filling the room with Leonard Cohen's voice. Ms. Kappl always plays the music she likes during recess. It would sound better if the kids outside would stop making so much noise. I look out the window. It's a sunny October afternoon, but I still don't want to go outside. I'm having trouble looking people in the eye today. Mummy and Daddy fought a lot last night and I yelled at them to stop. They yelled back at me so I ran up stairs and cried until I fell asleep. I think Ms. Kappl and my classmates can see how puffy my eyes are.

Maybe that's why she let me stay inside for recess again today.

I rub my right eye with my knuckles. After a few blinks, I catch sight of something fuzzy. Something with black and yellow stripes. Something dead. I rest my elbows on the windowsill. The sleeves of my pink hoodie protect my arms from the cold steel sill. I poke the fuzzy striped ball. It doesn't move.

"Ms. Kappl?"

"Yes, dear?" She looks up from the math tests and leans her gold-framed glasses on the tip of her nose.

"What do you think this is?"

She gets up from her desk. Her green and white floral print muumuu drags on the dusty tile floor. She kneels beside me.

"Oh my! Well that looks like a dead bee, Adelaide! I wonder how it got in here."

I lift my little hand to poke it again. She pokes it, too, but uses her long nail.

"Maybe it came in from the window." I point at the open crack of the window.

"That is definitely how it got in here. How sad that it had to die."

"What should we do with him, Miss?"

"Hmm." She gets up and walks over to the phone. Her long nail clicks against the plastic numbers as she dials.

"Hi, Mr. Gilruth, we have a bit of an emergency. There is a dead bee on our windowsill and it is in desperate need of a humane burial!" she says with urgency. Her pink cheeks turn a deeper shade of pink.

Mr. Gilruth is our janitor. He has long brown hair, a beard, and wears the same navy jumper every day. Ms. Kappl tells me she thinks he's cute.

She hangs up the phone, wipes her brow with the back of her hand in a dramatic swoosh, and places her hands on her wide hips.

"He's on his way!"

"Is he going to flush the bee down the toilet? That's what Daddy does with spiders when he finds one in the house."

"No, no! That is no way to go. We will bury him outside, where he belongs."

There's a knock on the door. Ms. Kappl scampers to the door, her muumuu dragging on the "Read Aloud" carpet.

"I hear there's an emergency?" Mr. Gilruth holds a dustpan and a brush.

"Yes, over there!"

Ms. Kappl points to me at the window. I kneel at the windowsill with my fuzzy friend.

"That one in the pink hoodie? She's too big to bury outside!"

I giggle. "No, Mr. Gilruth! The bee, the bee!"

He comes over to the windowsill. His worn brown work boots galumph on the tile floor, his heavy feet marching toward me. I look up.

Mr. Gilruth itches his scraggly beard and swipes the bee up with the brush. Dust bunnies, hair and lint hang off the bristles of the brush. The bee rolls onto the dustpan. Mr. Gilruth lifts it above my head. I clench my fists, scared the bee will fall on the floor.

"Alright, let's go bury this little guy," he says in his deep, scratchy voice.

Ms. Kappl and I follow Mr. Gilruth down the hall to his office. He opens the back door to a part of the yard kids aren't allowed to go during recess. There is a black wire fence covered in vines. They look liked the ones I was drawing earlier.

"Is here okay?" Mr. Gilruth kneels underneath the vine. Ms. Kappl gets close to him, her muumuu draping over the leaves of grass.

"Sure," I say.

"Wait! Before we bury him, we must give him a name. We can't have a funeral for a bee that has no name." Mr. Gilruth declares.

"Uhh..." I whisper.

"Think of something!" Ms. Kappl and Mr. Gilruth stare at me.

I think of the Leonard Cohen song that played in Ms. Kappl's classroom.

"Leonard." I smile.

"Alright, Leonard it is!"

Mr. Gilruth sweeps Leonard onto the ground underneath the big vine. He lays some stray leaves on top of Leonard's fuzzy striped body.

So long, Leonard.

Playing Cards

The phone on the wall rings. It interrupts Mrs. Kappl's second grade class.

I think it's for me.

Mum said something about a man, a meeting, and a phone call.

Ms. Kappl answers. We make eye contact. I rub the sweat off my palms onto my bare, scraped knees.

My heart sinks.

"Adelaide…" says Ms. Kappl. She nods her head at me and I get up.

The class falls silent. I can feel everyone's eyes watching me as I leave my desk.

I fiddle with the zipper on my purple velvet hoodie. I close the heavy door and walk down the stairs to my meeting. The stairwell smells like rubber, cement and orange peels.

I trudge down each step with heavy feet. I know the faster I get to the office, the faster I can leave. I exit the stairwell and enter the atrium. The sun shines through the glass ceiling and casts oversized shadows on the wrought-iron chairs and dusty fake plants. Screams and laughter from the kindergarteners across the hall seep through the windows of their classrooms. I listen to them as I stand outside the office.

I swing the office door open. I inhale hand sanitizer, dish soap and latex.

"Oh darlin' child, you must be Adelaide. Have a seat. He's comin' baby girl," the middle-aged secretary says.

She points to an empty seat beside a boy. His nose is bleeding. The secretary's wiry black hair frizzes out of her slicked back ponytail. She wipes excess blood off the boy's face with her slender ebony fingers.

I swing my legs back and forth. My feet do not touch the floor. My *Dora the Explorer* sneakers light up with each kick. I look up. A man who looks like Mr. Rogers, the star of one of my favourite shows, turns the corner of the office and disappears into another room.

"That's him baby girl you can go now. It's just down that hallway."

The secretary points toward Mr. Rogers with a blood-stained tissue in her hand. I smile at her and walk down the hall. I stop at a door that reads "Conference Room." It stands ajar. As I reach out a hand to grab the handle, I peek through the crack and see Mr. Rogers. He sits alone around a big table.

Mr. Rogers gets up from his chair and walks toward me.

"Well, you must be Adelaide. My name is Joe. I'm your social worker. It's a pleasure to meet you!" He extends his hand out to me.

I press my clammy hand into his and he shakes it as if I were a limp noodle. I sit in one of the big people chairs. My feet dangle again.

"So, can you think of why Mum and Dad wanted to get you a special person to talk to?" His voice startles me, as it breaks my fixed gaze on the floor. I look up. Mr. Rogers rolls up the sleeves of his wooly maroon sweater.

I shrug. "Uh, I don't know."

"Think about it," he says, his voice softens.

He even sounds like Mr. Rogers.

"Maybe because Mum and Dad don't get along?" I ask. He nods his head and smiles. "Or because I can't concentrate if I sit in class for too long? I don't really know, sir."

"Adelaide, please call me Joe."

"Okay."

"Well, you're right. Maybe talking about home will help you. And yes, I'm here to give you a break from class." He laughs. Mr. Rogers reaches into his pocket and pulls out a tattered deck of Bicycle playing cards.

"Okay Adelaide, let's get started. First off, from what your Mum and your teacher, Ms. Kappl tell me, I hear that you're very shy. I am going to ask you some things about home, but I understand if you're not completely comfortable or ready to open up ye--"

"Why do you have playing cards, sir?" I interrupt.

He smiles. "You'll find out soon."

"Okay, sorry."

"That's alright. Before we talk, I want you to know that anything you tell me will be confidential. I'm not gonna tell your parents. I'm not gonna tell your teachers. I'm pretty good at keeping secrets." He smiles again. "Okay, since this is our first session and we've never met, we should get to know each other." He rolls down his sleeves.

I nod.

"Okay, I'll start. I live alone with my Irish sheepdog. I like to do crosswords, golf and garden, and my favourite food is mac and cheese!"

"I like mac and cheese too, Joe."

"Good! We can be friends, then. Can you tell me some things you do in your spare time?"

I look at the floor. "Well, I like to draw pictures and read. Sometimes my little sister makes me play Barbies with her, but I don't really like Barbies. And sometimes I make up stories and draw them out on paper."

"I think these are all great things to do in your spare time."

"What time is it? Does Ms. Kappl want me to come back to class yet?" I kick my feet faster.

"Don't sweat it. Let the time pass. Since today is your first session with me, we don't have all that much to talk about. So now's a good time for me to show you why I brought these playing cards."

"Okay."

"We are going to play a card game called "Seven Up." Mr. Rogers takes a long time explaining the game, making sure I know exactly how to play. He shuffles the deck. He lays seven cards in front of the both of us.

The recess bell rings. Mr. Rogers and I play Seven Up while kids pour out of classrooms.

I win.

"Adelaide. Same time next week. Whenever you feel like you don't need me anymore, we'll stop these sessions, okay?"

"Okay. Thanks for playing with me."

I shift forward in the chair and reach my legs toward the tile floor. I run over to Mr. Rogers and hug him. His wooly sweater itches my cheek.

I run out of the office door and up the stairs to Ms. Kappl's classroom. I open the door. She sits at her desk and cuts apples out of red construction paper with pink grown-up scissors. Mrs. Kappl looks up and puts her scissors down.

"Why hello Miss Adelaide!" Her cheeks are as red as the construction paper. Her yellow floral patterned dress looks worn. It hugs her round body perfectly. I hope she lets me stay in for recess again today.

"Hi Miss, what are you making?" I ask her.

"It's for the student of the week activity I'm starting. Wanna help me cut stuff?"

"Yes please!"

"Okay, can you cut little leaves using green construction paper?" she slides a stack toward me.

I pick up a pair of purple safety scissors. I cut ovals the size of my pinky.

She cuts paper apples and does not look up. "How was your top secret meeting?"

"It was fun. The man I talked to looked like Mr. Rogers and asked me questions and played a card game with me."

"Really? You should teach me how to play sometime."

I cut more green ovals and put them in a pile. I have grown used to hearing the sound of kids playing outside, the soundtrack to my indoor recesses.

I stop cutting out ovals. "Ms. Kappl?"

"Yes, dear?"

"Is it okay that I'm staying in for recess a lot lately?"

"Of course it's okay, Adelaide. You are great company."

Shampoo

"Stop treating Ad the way your mother treated you! Stop ruining her confidence!" Dad roars.

Mum screams the loudest I've ever heard her.

I peek behind my bedroom door. Mum and Dad's door rests wide open.

"Dont you dare," she yells.

Wait, then who's giving Lexi a bath?

I swing my bedroom door open and bolt down the narrow hallway into my parent's master bathroom, rushing past the two un-lovers.

My sister sits in the middle of the bathtub in a pool of deflated bubbles. The air is heavy and humid. The white bath water is still.

"Sistie? What's going on?"

"It's alright, Lex. Let's get out of the tub, okay?"

I hold out my hand. Her shaky palm closes in mine. Her fingertips are cold and pruned. Lexi's foot squeaks against the tub as she tries not to slip.

I wonder how long she's been in there.

I tug a towel off the rod bolted to the wall. The only towels in the washroom are the towels with my parent's initials stitched in them: "C" for Connie, "A" for Alex. A wedding present from my Aunt.

"No, I can't get out! I still have shampoo in my hair!" Lexi touches the top of her head. Her hair is slick. As I lean next to her and wrap the towel around her cold body, the smell of coconut shampoo fills my nostrils.

"Lex, don't worry. It's not important. Just come with me to my room, come on."

We leave the bathroom. Lexi's knuckles turn white from squeezing mine. Her other hand holds the wedding towel around her small body. Dad screams indecipherable things at Mum as she shoves him against the wall. The bed frame crashes against the wall and slams against the nightstand. Mum's jewelry clatters on top of the dresser. Dad wraps his olive hands around her bone-coloured wrists, stopping her from her fierce slaps.

We reach my bedroom. I shove Lexi into my blue-walled sanctuary and look behind me. Mum whips Dad with a towel, the one we got from Malta last summer.

Lexi sits on the carpet with her towel half covering her shivering body.

I slam my door and kick, and kick, and kick.

"Adelaide, stop it!" Lexi cries. "You're going to break the door! You're gonna break it!"

"I'm sorry, Lex, I'm sorry." I kneel beside her and wrap the towel around her. She shivers.

"You know what, it's going to be okay, you know? They'll get tired eventually." I look at my Lizzie McGuire clock.

9:55pm.

"Are we going to school tomorrow?"

"I'm not sure Lex." I sit cross-legged beside her. "We'll have to see."

I jump to my feet and step over Lexi to get to my desk. I rip a corner off of a sketch I drew of Spongebob Squarepants. With a dull pink pencil crayon, I write: "No mean parents allowed. Sad kids only." I open the top drawer of my pine Ikea desk and grab a roll of tape. I burst outside my room and tape it to the door. I close it with another slam.

10:34pm.

Lexi and I sit on my unmade bed and play on our Tamogatchis. We don't speak.

There's a pounding on my bedroom door.

"We said no mean parents allowed! Can't you read?" Lexi yells as loud as a six-year-old can.

Dad opens the door. The sleeves of his Old Navy crewneck bunch around his forearms. The gold chain around his neck hides under his sweater. Dad's hazel eyes stare blankly at the ceiling, his pupils hollow. Mummy strolls in many feet behind him. Her leather belt sticks out of the denim loop of her worn jeans. Her copper hair has fallen out of place.

Dad pulls my yellow Ikea stool from under my desk and sits. Mum rests herself at the edge of my bed.

"Why are you two in my room? Can't you guys read?"

"Ad, Lex, we have to talk." Mum rubs the bridge of her nose and turns to us.

Lexi buries her face in her hands and cries. The towel falls to her waist.

Mum looks at Dad, purses her lips in a line and widens her eyes.

The room spins.

I hear dad say, "Guys, your mother and I have decided on a divorce."

My sister wails and holds her towel up. She tucks it under her armpits and leaps off my bed. She stomps over to my desk and walks around Dad, still sitting on my yellow stool. She picks up an extra piece of paper from a pile on my desk and starts to rip it into vertical strips.

"Daddy! This is my heart!" Lexi screams, her face red and wet. Snot drips out of her nose.

I hold back my tears.

I stand up and glare at my tired caregivers. Lexi and I walk out of my room and into our washroom. I slam the door behind me. Tears stream out of my eyes.

"Come on, Lex." I lean into the shower and turn the water on. "Let's get the shampoo out of your hair."

The Traveller

Of Giving and Goodbyes

March 10, 2011

I reach my hand around my back and unhook my bra. I place the blue bra I bought from Wal-Mart on top of the pile of clothing I've worn during my time in Guatemala. Worn clothes tower on top of each other on the bottom bunk – my bed.

I wore Wal-Mart bras for ten days. I want to leave them behind for the women of Jalapa.

The top bunk in "Room 1" creaks as Sara, my roommate, makes her bed. I hunch down and dodge the rod that holds the mattress up above me.

"Is everyone almost ready? Check all of the bathrooms! The showers. Other people's rooms. Leave anything here and you'll never see it again!" The shrill sound of Mrs. Pruchnicky's voice echoes throughout Camp Esperanza, our home for the last ten days.

All ten of us flow in and out of each other's rooms. I check the time on the plastic analog clock above the door of Room 1. *6:44 A.M.*

I walk into my room. Without ease, I throw my purple travel backpack on the bottom bunk. I slump onto my bed again and sit at the edge of the flimsy mattress. I put both arms through the straps and lunge forward.

Myself, my classmates and my teachers from St. Marcellinus Secondary School pile our luggage into the back of the *Wells of Hope* pickup truck. The sun creeps behind the mountains. I stand at the edge of the hill at Camp Esperanza, the camp that was our home for ten days, for the last time.

"Addy, let's go. We're gonna visit Virginia and then we have to catch our ten o'clock flight," Mr. Byrne, our school Chaplain, projects his voice as he pokes his head out of the passenger window. I turn around. All of my classmates pack together in the back of the vehicle. I climb up onto the truck and step over my classmates. The lack of space forces me to stand.

The yellow "Esperanza" sign grows smaller and smaller as we drive away from the camp.

I don't look back.

~~~

March 1, 2011

The sun beats down on my back in Jalapa, Guatemala. Heat radiates off the scrap metal panels that bind Virginia's house together. Droplets of sweat bead down my forehead. I squint while looking at Ted van der Zalm.

"This is Virginia. Her and her five children built this house together," Ted, the owner of *Wells of Hope* speaks to my classmates, teachers and I. Virginia stands at five feet, clad in a torn dress that swallows her frame. Her thick black hair is matted with dust, her face chapped.

How is this even legal?

I stand in front of a structure made from scraps of metal, large pieces of branch, and plastic garbage bags. My brand new hiking boots sink into the mud that surrounds the house. Dead trees and bushes hide the property.

Virginia lives with her five children and her ex-husband's mother in a shack the size of a public washroom. The shack has two beds and is cluttered with dirty pots, old plastic bottles and broken toys. Two single beds lay beside each other. Tattered flannel blankets cover each bed.

"Today, the Lord has sent us on a mission. The Lord sent us to Virginia to help her and her family. We will take this house apart and begin to dig trenches around the grounds to construct the foundation. Clear?" Ted wipes his sweaty forehead with his muddy white tank top. He turns his gaze away from us and speaks to Virginia in Spanish.

Virginia leans against the metal panels of her house. She begins to cross herself and repeat, "Santa Maria."

"Everyone listen up! Let's begin disassembling the house." Ted's dirty forefinger points to buckets. "There are tools over here for snipping wires and cutting ropes."

I reach my hand into one of the buckets. I pull out a pair of pliers with my turquoise nailpolished fingers and begin to snip chords and ropes that bind the structure together. Virginia's daughter unhooks a small picture of the Virgin Mary and baby Jesus from a branch.

"Jesucristo, nos da fuerza. Velar por nosotros Jesús," *Jesus Christ gives us strength. Jesus watch over us.* She holds the picture to her chest, closes her eyes and rocks back and forth, "Jesucristo, nos da fuerza. Velar por nosotros Jesús," she chants. I walk over to her.

"Hola cariño, cual es tu nombre?" I reach out my hands. She crawls into my arms, still grasping the picture.

Of Giving and Goodbyes

"Hola," she says in a hushed voice. "Mi nombre es Daisy."

"Well, Daisy, tu casa," I point at the shack, now a skeleton of branches and wires, "we make…bigger…better." I gesture grandiose hand motions toward her broken home.

Daisy smiles at me as she sits on my lap, still clutching the picture of Jesus. "Si! Grande?"

"Si, Daisy, grande!"

We throw the remaining parts from Virginia's house in a pile near a dead tree. As we take apart the structure, we remove the family's belongings. I bend down and pick up a naked, muddy Barbie doll. She sits atop one of the two cots. I take Barbie over to the water dispenser and rinse her off. Her hair, her joints and her nostrils are all caked with mud.

I look at the mud. White spray paint surrounding the property marks where we have to dig. The hot midday sun mixes with dust, smoke from fires, and dirt that makes it difficult to breathe. Daisy and her siblings joyously play with their skinny Jack Russel terrier. The heads of my classmates are shielded with straw hats and promotional ball caps. Everyone's clothes are covered in soil.

~~~

I can feel the heat on my shoulders. I realize I forgot to apply sunscreen this morning. I continue digging in hopes that it will distract me from my fresh sunburn. My back begins to ache from all the hunching I've been doing for the past three hours. My chest tightens up and I begin to cough.

Shit, my puffer.

I lean my shovel on a tree and walk toward our backpacks. I begin to rummage through my bag in search for my puffer. *Shit*. I continue coughing.

"Addy, you okay?" Mr. Byrne walks toward me. His face is red and covered in sweat. His blue "Jesus Saves, Bro," shirt sticks to his hefty body, and his thinning brown hair sticks to his forehead.

"Yeah, I just need my puffer and it's not in my bag. I guess I left it back at camp."

"It's okay man, sit out for a bit. The Lord understands."

I let out a nervous laugh and sit alone at a rotting picnic table. Red ants crawl up the table's gray wooden legs.

Half an hour goes by. I watch as my classmates dig deeper and deeper into the now-dry soil. I chug the warm remains from my tin water bottle and put my dusty gloves back on. I retrieve my shovel from the dead tree.

~~~

"Okay, listen up!" Ted balances one foot on the edge of his shovel and rests both hands on the tip of the handle. "We are done for the day. Our goal is to finish Virginia's house in the next nine days. I know we can do it! Tomorrow, we lay the bricks. Gather your things and make your way back to the truck."

As I collect my things and shove them into my backpack, I see Virginia. She stands alone. She looks at the wreckage of what used to be her home. Piles of iron boards, sticks, leaves and rope lay in a messy pile. Daisy and her older siblings' laughter become greater as they run across the property towards their mother.

Daisy stops. Her brow furrows, staring at the same decapitated piles of infrastructure. She hugs her mother's leg.

"Mami, mirar a nuestra casa." *Mommy, look at our house.* Daisy hides behind Virginia, her squeaky voice muffled as she speaks into the worn hem of her mother's dress.

Virginia pats Daisy's dirt-caked pigtails and whispers in Daisy's ear. "Niña, al mal tiempo, buena cara."

Daisy does not let go of her mother. Virginia tells her

daughter, *My child, put a good face to the bad times.*

A single tear runs down Daisy's face. The tear leaves a visible line through the powdery dirt caked on her cheek. She wipes her face on her mother's dress, smudging the wet tear in with the dried mud. Her mother stares down at Daisy, rubbing the filth off her daughter's face with a dry, cracked thumb.

Virginia and her family stay with her sister in the closest village.

~~~

March 10, 2011

The bumpy car ride to Virginia's was a quiet one. The sun hangs in the white sky. I place a hand over my brows, shield my face from the morning sun, and hold on to the hood of the truck. My nine classmates and I say nothing to each other.

The gravel crunches under the truck's tires as we drive up the path to Virginia's. Everyone stumbles and bumps into each other while holding old grocery bags full of used clothing. The bags read, "Gracias, Supermercado La Torre" *Thank you, from, Supermarket Tower* in bold red letters. We leave our belongings in the truck and follow Ted up the dirt path.

"I'm gonna miss this walk," my friend Ayla says, eyes focused on her hiking boots.

"I know, girl. I still can't believe it's been ten days already." I swing my plastic bag full of clothes back and forth as I walk.

I look at what was a structure made of tin, plastic and sticks ten days ago and at what was a muddy trench seven days ago. Now, a small rectangular house made from muddy bricks stands in its place. Virginia, Daisy and her siblings sit at the withering picnic table. Daisy runs toward Ayla and I.

"Hola little sweetness!" Ayla croons.

"Buenos días, Daisy. ¿Cómo estás" I say as Daisy presses our sunburned faces against her chapped cheeks.

We peel Daisy off of us. I look up at the sun and hope it will dry the tear sliding down my cheek. I wipe it off with the back of my hand. Ayla runs toward the picnic table and places her plastic bag with the others. I stare at the little brick building that stands on Virginia's piece of land. There is no door, just a frame in the building for entry.

"Brothers and Sisters in Christ," Ted projects his voice even though we are two feet away from him, "look what we've created together. Look what God gave us. Mud to make bricks. People to lay them. Hardworking students and teachers to build a house for this beautiful family. I hope you can all recognize what a large effect you've had on this family's lives. And for that, I thank you." Clapping breaks the silent pause. I look over at Daisy. Her little mud-caked hands clap together as she looks up at her mother and smiles.

Virginia and her children rummage through the bags. Virginia pulls the blue bra out of my grocery bag. She holds it up to her chest and smiles. Virginia looks around and puts it back in the bag. Daisy pulls a handful of Barbie dolls out of Ayla's contribution.

"Daisy…pretty…like you!" Ayla sits at the picnic table. She places Daisy on her lap and brushes the Barbie's hair with her slender pale fingers. I join Ayla and watch as Daisy's little smile grows wider with each Barbie she holds.

"Five minutes guys, we don't want to miss our flight!" Ted commands.

I look at Daisy as she holds her new Barbies close to her chest.

I go up to Virginia.

"Virginia, gracias por todo," *Thank you for everything*, I say as she pulls me close and kisses me on the cheek.

She whispers in my ear, "Mi cariño, la fe mueve montañas."

My darling, faith will move mountains.

Joy

I sit alone on a bus seat for two. It is late in the afternoon on February 15, 2015 in Vancouver, British Columbia. I soak in the feeling of freedom on the second day of my solo vacation. I scroll through my phone as the bus passes down Robson Street. I hear a web of conversations tangling around me. Vance Joy sings "Georgia" to me through my headphones. I turn my music up louder to drown out the conversations.

I am on my way to see the childhood home of my favourite Canadian author, Joy Kogawa – a woman who was brave enough to resurface her family's past during the Japanese Internment, and put it into words. I never thought I would have the chance to meet her.

I hope she's home.

I step off of the bus to Granville Street as it stops at 63rd Avenue West. The sun peeks through the oak trees that tower over the bus stop. The hot scent of after rainfall hangs in the air. I walk down the sidewalk toward run down local shops and restaurants. I pass a store called Vera's Burger Shack. The slogan reads, "You can't beat Vera's meat." A red "For Lease" sign covers the last few letters of the slogan. Across the street, a blinking sign with red, yellow and green lights reads, "Fresh Sushi". I walk down 64th Avenue West. Ordinary houses are placed in neat rows. I open Google Maps on my iPhone and type in the address. It directs me further down the street filled with ordinary houses. "Your destination will be on your right," the app says.

I look to my right and do not see the Joy Kogawa House, her property does not stand out from the rest: each residency hides behind rows of trees. Fourteen fifty is her address so I search for the number.

1442, 1446, 1448, 1450. 1450. *This must be it.*

I stare at the house from across the sidewalk. It is no bigger than the house I grew up in in Mississauga, the house I left once Mum moved out. It is much bigger than the house I helped build while in Jalapa, Guatemala.

The stucco gray and black property stands in front of me from across the sidewalk. I look through the two little windows below the roof. This is the window that three-year-old Joy looks out of on the cover of her famous book, "Obasan." She peers through the raindrops on the window, with short jet black hair and rosy cheeks. I wish I could tell three-year-old Joy that this will all end soon, just as I told to Daisy when we tore her home from its roots.

"Obasan" was a book I read in second year for a Canadian Short Story class. I went to Dr. Hill, my Canadian Literature professor's, office hours to discuss Kogawa's novel. That's when he told me she lives in Vancouver. I decided I would visit while vacationing here.

In her book, Joy wrote about living in West Vancouver with her family during the Japanese Internment. While looking at this house, I remember a quote from the story said by her grandmother; "Kodomo no tame," meaning "for the sake of the children," in Japanese. The thought of hiding your family's history from future generations makes me think of my own family – if I didn't know about our past, I would not know what my family went through. A piece of me would be missing.

If I look deeper through the windows, I can imagine three-year-old Joy walking away from the dingy, rain-streaked casement and back into the attic. But now that I am here, I don't know what to do. I didn't think Joy would be here, but I'm curious who is.

Do I knock?
What if nobody answers?
What if they do answer, what would I say?

I look down at my scuffed Keds. The saliva in my mouth dries up. I look far down the street and see a sign for a coffee shop. I decided to walk down the street and get an iced tea. Maybe by then I'll build up the courage to knock.

I walk down the street. It had just finished raining this morning so the air smells of worms and wet mulch. I watch where I step. Little packs of worms squirm around on the now-dry cement sidewalk. The air is hot and muggy, so I take my flannel shirt off and tie it around my waist.

As I enter a coffee shop called Browns Socialhouse, leather chairs full of locals scatter around the room. Soft jazz plays from the speakers overhead and is accompanied by the clanking of tin milk pitchers. I walk up to the cashier. I look above the barista. The menu board lists classic café beverages in smudged chalk.

"Can I just have an iced tea?"

"Sure" She smiles.

I reach to the bottom of my shoulder bag and fish out a five-dollar bill.

Joy

I retrieve my iced tea from the bar and sit in an empty leather chair. I look at the time on my phone. I scroll through my phone and Google the "Joy Kogawa House." Kogawa-house.com says it was turned into a space for writers to hold workshops, as well as a "literary landmark and symbol of hope, healing and reconciliation for all Canadians." I read this a few times and think to myself. *Just knock, the worst thing that could happen is the house owner tells you to leave.*

I gather my things and exit the café.

I walk past the worms writhing in the sun on 64th Avenue West until I'm facing the small historic house. I carefully step up the broken-down stairs to the porch. The staircase creaks.

Is this trespassing?

I bet she's short and soft-spoken. I wonder if she has children. I'm going to tell her how much I love her writing.

No, wait, is that creepy?

Saliva dries up again. I wipe my shoes on the "Welcome" mat. It looks just like the one Mum has on her porch. I knock. As I wait, I peer through the window beside the porch. A simple lady, who probably runs the workshops sits at the kitchen table and talks the phone. She doesn't look up. I rock back and forth on my heels. *I bet she is busy.*

I wait in silence.

I walk down the creaky staircase and toward the sidewalk. I leave the solitary house behind me. The scent of rain, tempura, and hot cement grow stronger the closer I get to the bus stop. I look back at the house. Clouds form over the mountains in the distance. The trees sway back and forth, as if to wave goodbye. With the same gust of wind, it starts to rain.

Maybe it's better she wasn't there.

Esther

I stand in the kitchen of my great Auntie Esther's hundred-year-old home in Qormi, Malta. The air is stuffy and warm with the smell of traditional Maltese pastries, pastizzis. The buttery scent of the flaky pastry mixes with the warm ricotta cheese in the pastizzi. It smells just like Nanna's house.

"One for il *gbira*, one for iz *zghira*." My great Aunt Esther hands Lexi and I ten euros each. Gbira means big and zghira means little.

"Grazzi, Zi," Thank you, Auntie.

"Now go buy yourself some *qliezet ta taht*." She tells us to get new underwear.

"Okay, Zi, we promise." Lexi laughs.

"No more candy floss like the ones I washed this morning," Auntie Esther says as she smacks her hand on top of the green vinyl kitchen table.

We walk outside. Our colourful thongs slowly sway on the clothesline on the roof. Auntie Esther hung them there this morning. Small dingy clothespins hold them down to dry in the hot summer wind. Lexi and I sit on the *bitha*, the patio built into Auntie Esther's house. The walls are made of white limestone. The blue mosaic tiles on the *bitha* huddle together.

We look out at Auntie Esther's garden. Dried cracked mud fills the yard. A drooping vegetable garden dies of dehydration. Dad always told me about the plump, pink bougainvillea flowers and red rose bushes tucked away in the garden, and how Auntie Esther watered them diligently.

But now, the bushes are nothing but skeletons, the bones of a once blooming rose bush. Just like Nannu's.

Flip-flops clack on the tile floor. Auntie Esther pulls a tin patio chair out from underneath the round table and eases into it, hanging onto the edge of the table. She places a pastizzi wrapped in a napkin on the patio table. Flakey pastry bits sprinkle to the ground. Auntie Esther adjusts her thick black glasses and glances in the distance, as if she's looking for something.

"*Fejek*, Shoosha?" *Where's my cat, Shoosha?* Auntie Esther makes kissing noises. "Shoosha, Shoosha!"

A white Persian cat with a flat face and dirt-caked paws slowly struts toward us like a lion approaching its prey.

"Shoosha, there you are," Auntie Esther says as she picks up Shoosha and places her on her lap. Shoosha sways her tail back and forth as Auntie Esther pets her. The cat looks like Lucifer from Cinderella.

"I save her from the wild, you know."

"Zi, is that safe?" Lexi asks.

"Oh aeya! Of course." She picks Shoosha up like Rafiki lifts Simba in *The Lion King*.

She sets her down.

"You know," Auntie Esther continues, "I save her from the wild."

Lexi and I look at each other.

"Uhm, yeah you tol--" I kick Lexi's leg under the table.

"That's nice of you, Zi. Where from the wild?"

"I don't remember," Auntie Esther says, scratching her puffy orange-dyed hair. For the first time, I notice she doesn't wear a wedding ring.

Auntie Esther shuffles into the kitchen. Flip-flops slap the tiles. She turns around as if she left something on the table.

"You want pastizzi?"

"No thank you, Zi," Lexi and I both reply.

The front door creaks open. Nanna, Nannu and Dad walk through. As Lexi and I approach the door, I peel my backside off the sticky vinyl patio seat. I open the screen door to the sunroom and walk down a short hallway toward the lobby, where Nanna, Nannu and Dad stand. Pictures of Nanna, Auntie Esther and Auntie Jessie scatter across the limestone walls. Auntie Jessie passed away years ago. The three sisters wear colourful 1950s dress suits. Nanna is the tallest one at 5 feet. A single vase with a fake rose sits atop a *bitzilla*, a traditional lace doily. The vase and *bitzilla* rest on a dusty cherry wood side table.

"Okay girls, we're going back to our hotel. Buggiba is a twenty minute drive so we should leave now if we want to be on time for dinner," Nannu says.

His white "Walk for the Cure 2010" shirt sticks to his toned, sweaty body. He puts his black sunglasses on top of a bed of gray hair. Nanna stands behind him.

"Did you thank Zi Esther?" Dad asks.

Lexi runs to Auntie Esther, feet sticking to the tile floor. I follow.

We double kiss Auntie Esther on the cheek, crouching down to reach her.

"Aeya, wait!" she shuffles over to the cherry coffee table in the living room. Lace curtains create little windows of light through the patterns on the wall. She unbuttons her purse.

"Before you go, take this." Auntie Esther fans a handful of euros and plucks two tens. "One for *gbira*, one for *zghira*."

Lexi and I pause. Lexi looks at Dad and points at another ten-euro bill sticking out of the back pocket of her ripped jean shorts.

"Well, take it! Go buy yourself some *qliezet ta taht*."

I nod my head and take the second bill.

"Thank you, Zi." I kiss her cheek. "We'll be sure to buy new underwear."

~~~

Nanna, Lexi and I squish in the backseat of the van that Nannu rented. Dad joins him in the front seat. We cruise down unpaved roads, passing through dusty plains. We pass old limestone buildings covered in thick vines and surrounded by large rocks. Huge Aleppo Pine trees stand in rows on either side of the road. The clear blue sky allows the sun to be alone. My hairline beads with sweat. So does Lexi's. Nanna doesn't sweat. She's used to Malta's heat.

"Aeya, dad, look!" Dad points out the window of the rickety van. "A fruit stand!"

Nannu signals left and pulls over. The two men get out of the car.

Lexi looks at me, and then Nanna. Nanna holds on to the handle attached to the car ceiling and looks out the window on the right side.

"Nanna?" Lexi says.

"Yes, *Pupa*." Nanna looks away from the window.

"Zi gave us ten euros two separate times." Lexi pulls the bills from her back pocket.

"Yeah, I didn't know what to say," I add, pulling the bills out of my back pocket.

We place them on our laps.

Smoke and Roses

Nanna looks out the window.

"When your daddy was small," Nanna says, letting go of the handle and folding her hands on her lap, "we would sit in the kitchen at Auntie Esther's, and she would order people around like nobody's business." Nanna's accent rings through her words. "She would tell people, 'do this, do that!' and your daddy looked at her and said, 'Zi, are you the boss of this house?' And everyone start to laugh! She said, 'Yes, Alex, I *am* the boss of this house!'"

Lexi and I undo our seatbelts and turn our bodies toward Nanna. Tears well in her hazel eyes. Her wrinkles bunch up around the corners.

"She was the boss." Nanna sniffles, her voice breaking. "She was the assistant to the Prime Minister of Malta. She held the family together like you would not imagine. We would gather at her house during the summer."

Nanna continues. "When I was a baby, my sisters and I would go underground in a huge tunnel that they dug. Nazi Germany's planes would fly above and start bombing Malta. I would cry and cry and Esther would rock me until I stopped. We squished under there for hours until it was safe."

"In that exact house?" Lexi asks.

"Yes." Nanna pulls a wad of tissue from her pocket and wipes her eyes. "The exact house where we grew up. It's just so hard to see my sister like this now."

Nanna looks out the window and wipes her eyes.

"To see her giving you ten euros twice and asking the same question over and over… She was my best friend. Now I can't help her. I can't watch her like this, I can't…" Nanna cries harder.

"Well Uncle Antoine takes care of her, and she has Shoosha," I say, rubbing Nanna's warm back.

"She would be nowhere without Antoine. She's so lost. She forgets to wash sometimes." Nanna sniffles. "I can't come to Malta anymore."

"Oh Nanna, don't say that. This is your home!" Lexi says.

"It's just hard to see my sister like this."

Tears run down Nanna's wrinkled cheeks. Lexi pats her leg and looks at me. She reaches for my hand and I squeeze her palm in mine. I imagine Lexi and myself in the future, who we'll become and how we'll treat each other. We sit holding hands until Dad and Nannu return to the van.

Houston's

I adjust my blue v-neck t-shirt that reads "Team Bride" across my chest in gold letters. I don't need anyone staring down my shirt tonight.

A medley of trashy top 40 songs and country singles blare from the sound units sprawled across Houston's Country Bar in Brandon, Manitoba. Cigarette smoke lingers in the air.

"To Catherine getting hitched," shouts Colin, one of Cat's best friends, as he raises a dripping shot of tequila in the air.

I look at the wedding party to see if they're looking at me. I pound the shot of rubbing alcohol flavoured liquid. My face scrunches. I bring the last lime on the tray up to my teeth, bite, and squeeze.

My Keds stick to the tarnished hardwood as I walk down the stairs to join the wedding party on the dance floor. Ryan, Cat's old friend from gymnastics leads the way into the crowd. I follow his tall blond head into the pool of sweaty strangers. Stale, muggy air makes it hard to breathe.

What a bad time to forget my puffer.

We find Cat with a drink in each hand, dancing to "Watch Me Nae Nae." She wears a white v-neck t-shirt that reads

"Bride" in gold letters and a ripped pair of white jeans. On top of her head, a pink fuzzy crown with plastic dicks and gems glued onto it bounces with each dance move. It matches the dick décor in our hotel room at the Royal Oak Inn and Suites, one of the only hotels in Wheat City Brandon.

"Hey bitch!" she screams over "Chicken Fried" by Zac Brown Band. People in plaid shirts and worn Bass Pro Shop hats brush my shoulders and dance around me. Beer and B.O. mingle on the stuffy dance floor.

"Hey Dick Queen." I laugh. "Double fisting the drinks, are we?"

"You bet." Cat shoves a straw from each glass into her mouth and sips. "You feelin' okay? I know you want to hermit right now, but I hope you're having fun."

She knows me too well.

"No, I'm actually okay."

"Here, have this." She hands me one of her drinks with a chewed pink straw inside. "Whiskey sour. Your favourite."

I take the drink, push the straw aside with my nose, and chug it.

"Yas! That's my best friend! Go best friend!"

Cat grabs my wrist. "I have to use the washroom. Come."

We shove past the crowd of people making out, line dancing and grinding. A few pairs of cowboy boots step on my toes. My t-shirt brushes against flannels and tight dresses. I stumble up the stairs into the washroom. Signs promoting the next Houston's events crowd the wood-paneled wall.

"Houston's Country Roadhouse Blackout Friday! September 18, 2015. Free cover, all drinks $4.50."

Cat kicks the door open with her white Converse. All the stalls are taken except for one.

"Come in with me," she says as she tugs my wrist into

the lonely stall. I walk over puddles and stray pieces of toilet paper. The air mixes with piss and perfume. Girls zhush their hair and pretend to wash their hands in front of the finger-printed mirrors.

Cat slides her white jeans around her ankles. A bright pink thong follows. As she sits down, a blowjob shot, a tequila shot, three mixed drinks and a lemonade pours out of her. I stand in front of her, palms against the stall door. I adjust her crown, tangled in her long blond hair.

"Thanks, bitch." She looks up at me. "Yo, thank you for being my bridesmaid. Thank you for coming all the way to my hometown to celebrate the biggest day of my life with me. I'm glad we get to snuggle in Grandma's spare room. She would have loved you."

"Of course babe. I am honoured to be a bridesmaid. And I know, I would have loved her too. She's with us, though. And she'll be with you when you say 'I do' tomorrow."

A black tear slides down her pale face and falls onto her hot pink lips.

She sniffles. "And thanks for being a champ. You're my best friend. I know you hate clubs and people, but I hope you're having fun. We just need to get a few more drinks in you." She pulls up her pants and buttons them around her hips.

"And you're my best friend," I say.

I unlock the stall door and join half drunk girls in heels at the sinks. Cat looks at her reflection through the barely visible mirror.

"Bro, I look like a hot mess."

"Who gives a shit, who are you trying to impress?"

As Cat and I approach the washroom door, two girls in tight pink dresses stop us. A girl with straight black hair and a silver cellophane sash that reads "Birthday Queen" speaks.

"Oh my fucking god. I love this crown," she says, as she touches the pink plastic dicks.

"Thanks, I'm getting married tomorrow and my best friends and I are celebrating my bachelorette."

"Oh shit, you're getting married!" Birthday Queen shrieks. "What's the secret?"

"Find yourself a good Christian man."

The two girls laugh. "Pfffft! Fuck that!"

They storm out and disappear into the sea of drunk Manitoba folk.

We shove through the crowd on the dance floor and stumble up the stairs to the bar. Cat shoves through people lounging at the bar and shouts, "Two pornstars please!"

The tall blonde bartender with crooked teeth slides two shot glasses full of bright blue liquid across the metal countertop.

"To my best friend's last night before being a married woman!" I clank the tiny glass against hers. We down the sour candy liquid in unison and slam the glasses on the counter.

The Woman

Selfish

Dear Adelaide (my first baby),

    I am not going to stop you from going to live with your father. I'm also not going to lie and tell you I'm okay with it. Yes, I was angry, and yes, I'm a little hurt. It makes me wonder what I have done wrong. If the fact that I don't have a lot of money is the problem, then you should know I gave you what I could. Daddy says you talked to counselors at school to discuss this and I am glad they were there for you.

    I will learn to be fine with this, but you are neglecting one person: your sister. Sisters are supposed to grow up together. If you leave, there is one thing I ask of you. You cannot let Lexi think this is her fault. She's just 13.

    So make your decision knowing I will not stop you or make it difficult.

I love you,
Mum xoxo

~~~

Mrs. Giovanni, my high school counselor at St. Marcellinus Secondary School, slides a box of one-ply tissues over to me.

"I just don't want to make my Mum sad," I say. Tears run down my face like the rain droplets on the industrial window of Mrs. Giovanni's office.

"I know, but sometimes, you have to be selfish." She tucks a curly black lock of hair behind her ear.

"I just can't get anything done. The TV is always on. Mum and Lexi are always fighting. The walls are paper-thin. The house is always a mess. There's no peace."

"And you said earlier that this is affecting your grades?"

"Yeah, I keep getting 60s because I can't concentrate through the yelling and my sister's Worst Top 40 playlists."

"How do you think your sister's going to feel?"

I bury my face in my hands and shake my head.

Tears. Again.

"I don't wanna think about it. It's hard though because she always steals my things. Nothing's sacred. Nothing's mine."

"But that's just what sisters do."

My hands slide down my men's polyester uniform pants.

I wipe the corners of my eyes with both index fingers. "Yeah, but that doesn't mean I have to be okay with it."

"Oh, your makeup's running," she says as she slides me the box of tissues.

"I know." I dab my face. Clumps of mascara and CoverGirl foundation a shade too dark for me smear across the rough tissue. "How am I going to move my things out without her noticing?"

"Just do it gradually. When you go to your dad's for the weekend, bring a little extra. Then just leave that stuff there."

I look out the office window. Through the droplet-covered pane, Ms. Abruzzi's third period gym class does laps around the school's two million dollar football field.

"Okay darling, I think you've had enough for one day. Tell

you what – I'm going to call Mr. DeLuca and tell him that you won't be returning to math class for personal reasons." The sun hits her sparkly engagement ring. It twinkles as she dials the numbers on the phone.

"Thank you, Mrs. Giovanni."

Slowly, I shut the door to her office. *At least I get to miss the torture that is grade eleven math.* I walk to the bus stop in front of the Courtney Park Library and wait for the 61N Mississauga Transit bus.

~~~

I open the fridge. Week old celery, lemonade and cheese strings sit sporadically around the skeleton shelves. I sigh and close the fridge.

I rush up the stairs and into my room. My empty stomach follows me. Light peeks through the shutters and creates patterns on my mint green walls. On my closet door, Kurt Cobain's black and white eyes fixate on the kitten balancing on his arm as he sits cross-legged on a bed of Seattle grass. I slide the beach tote Dad bought me two years ago, when we lived in Oakville with his god-awful girlfriend, out of my closet. He thought getting personalized colourful canvas beach totes would make going back and forth less difficult on my sister and I. She got a pink one. I got a blue one.

I run my fingers over the *Adelaide* in white cursive stitched lettering. I sit cross-legged on the carpeted floor of my room, still in my black and red uniform.

My "Dark Side of the Moon" Pink Floyd Shirt: Check.
My glow in the dark SpongeBob pajama bottoms: Check.
My Tiffany's necklace from Grandma: Check.
My sketchbook: Check.

I pile everything into the Divorce Bag. I roll up each piece of clothing into tight logs, stacking each shirt, tank top and pair of pajamas on top of each other. I push my clothes further and further into the bag to make the most out of the little room I have.

As I head toward the stairs, I step over the clothes, underwear, and bras that spill out of Lexi's doorway.

I walk into Mum's room and pause. I sit on the purple couch near her window. Pillows made from old colourful silk Saris swallow me. The mirrored sequins scratch the backside of my uniform pants. As the stale smell of last night's incense fills my nose, I scan the room. *Should I take something before I go? A pair of her earrings? Her Eeyore pajama shirt? The picture of her and I at Springridge Farm?*

Behind a frame, two-year-old me sits on Mum's lap. She stares at her redheaded toddler through dark circular sunglasses. Behind us are green hills. Smiling, my tiny hands grip the stationary tractor's steering wheel.

I grip the plastic black frame and throw it in my bag. I hope she doesn't mind I took it with me; this is Mum's favourite picture of us.

I lock the front door and rest the bag on my forearm.

As rain litters the streets, I walk to Dad's. His move back to Mississauga made going back and forth more convenient, but no less frustrating.

"Hello?" I say as I open the door to my Dad's house. The smell of lemon from yesterday's visit from the cleaning ladies mingles with the smell of rain.

No answer. He must still be at work.

I toss the bag on the tile floor in the doorway and unzip my black TNA coat. I bolt upstairs.

"Reeeeerwwmm!" Sounds from the gray kitty Dad bought me come from his room. I inch toward the doorway of Dad's master bedroom. The carpet is etched with fresh vacuum marks. A pile of suit jackets with dry cleaner tags lay on his King sized bed. The forced grocery store family photo we took last year sits atop his cherry wood wardrobe. No dust. Framed pictures of my sister and I collect on his dresser. The same bedroom set from our old house sits sporadically around his room. Hugo Boss watches and his collection of rosaries gather on his dresser.

I lay on the floor and pet our gray cat on his whiskery cheek. He rubs his fluffy self against my pant leg.

"Hi Levon, hi baby!"

Down the hall, I open the door to my room. Just as I left it. My blue and brown Roxy bed sheets rest crookedly across my bed. Brown wheels hold up my mattress. It looks like a 1970s hospital bed frame. I wouldn't be surprised if it was. The walls are painted baby blue. My "Dark Side of the Moon" poster hangs on the wall with tape. Aunt Sue's old white furniture from the 1980s crowd my room. On my dresser are half burned vanilla candles. A matted Coke stain sinks into my beige carpet, still there from the 15th birthday sleepover I had a year and a half ago.

I unload my Mary Poppins bag of items into my empty shell of a dresser. After unloading my stuff, the Divorce Bag sits deflated in the corner of my room.

Sun gleams through my window as the rain subsides.

The rain stops, as if God turned a tap to the left.

My BlackBerry Curve vibrates on my dresser. I leap to check who texted me.

Mum: 2:33pm: Hi baby, where are you?
~*Addy*~: 2:33pm: Just at Dad's. Might be here for a while.

0.1%

I open her journal to the first page.

Journal Entry 1
September 5, 2014

We're all a little broken, aren't we? I used to have this profound idea that I could change the world. And if not the world, at least a few people in it.

I remember sitting in the Doctor's chair thinking I would never be the one. I look in the mirror, thinking this powerful disease is trying to take over. But I will not let it. Some days I feel hopeless and I can't help but cry. But I am lucky to be breathing.

I remember sitting in the emergency room. I thought all was well. Then a doctor with a clipboard spoke: "We're sorry, but this is 99.9% lymphoma." That pit stuck in my throat stayed there with the 0.1% that it isn't true, 0.1% that it's all a dream.

I cried about the little things like losing my hair and gaining weight. I didn't want to tell anyone because I was scared I was going to be treated differently.

But then Addy told me: "You're still the same Maddie, just in a different location." She's right.

When I sit in the chemo room, I watch how excited people get after taking two bites of a sandwich without vomiting. I am not one of those people yet.

The thing about cancer is that it boils its own emotions. It engulfs inside me and turns me sour. Jealousy surfaces and the loneliness becomes indescribable.

My life has stopped and I know I'm missing out. But I know it will soon be over.

I don't know if I'll survive, but I know I can fight.

Cancer, I will beat you.

~~~

August 8, 2014

I sit on my bed and read Kurt Vonnegut's *Cat's Cradle*. My iPhone rings.

It's Ayla.

"Hey, Addy?"

"Ayla? What's up?" I pause and wait for an answer. "Are you crying?"

She sniffles. "Uhm, yeah. Listen, Addy, Maddie called me with some bad news."

"Uhm." I pause. I swallow the lump in my throat. "What happened?"

Ayla bursts into tears. "Maddie has cancer. Lymphoma."

I look up at the ceiling. The room spins. Tears flow out of my eyes. Maddie, the active, healthy one. The goofy one. The youngest one. At sixteen, Maddie is the one who is not influenced by what others think.

I pause, wipe the tears off my cheeks and reply. "When did you find this out?"

"When you were in Cuba a few days ago. I'm sorry for telling you the bad news, but Maddie's Mom and sister are not in a good place right now," she says through exhausted whimpers.

"Okay Ail, I'm gonna call you back. Love you."

I rush to my Dad's room. He lies in his king sized bed and watches another hockey game. Mascara runs down my cheek like little rivers. I lie on his stomach and begin to bawl.

"Ad, what happened?" He shoots his gaze away from the television.

"Maddie Curtis has cancer." I wail.

He jolts up, sitting upright in his bed. "What?"

"Ayla just called me and told me that Maddie has cancer."

"Ad, I'm sorry." He wraps his arms around me and squeezes me tight, the kind of hug he has given me since I was a little girl. "What kind is it?"

"Lymphoma." I sniffle. "When should I tell Lexi? When she comes home from the cottage? Now?"

"Don't do it now. Wait until she gets home."

He holds me until the tears run out.

~~~

Ayla and I pile out of our best friend Daniel's Volkswagen Jetta as he pulls up in front of The Hospital for Sick Children. Ayla and I inch toward the sliding doors of the hospital. As we walk in, the smell of cigarette smoke and diesel turn into hand sanitizer and latex.

In the lobby is a food court, the kind you'd see at a mall. An elevator stands in the middle of the hospital surrounded by windows on each of the eight levels. The windows look like the windows in a greenhouse. Small trees grow in giant pots all around the lobby. The trees look like an attempt to turn the sterile environment into a forest, providing fresh air.

I grip a coil notebook close to my chest. Positive quotes are glued onto the cover of a 250-page workbook I bought from the dollar store. They read: "Turn the pain into power." "You may see me struggle but you'll never see me quit." "If I can still breathe I'm fine." "Wear your tragedies like armour," and the like. My Introduction to Expressive Writing professor told me, "Writing can help heal the sick."

This is my contribution to the fight.

"She said she was on the seventh floor." Ayla checks her phone, holding a bouquet of baby pink roses in her arms. She swings her long brown hair over her shoulder. Daniel catches up with us. His skinny frame runs toward the elevator, his car keys jangling in his palm as he runs.

"What floor is she on?" He doesn't even pant.

"Seven," Ayla answers.

I follow my friends into the elevator. We rise above the lobby. Through the glass on each floor, I see pale tired children in wheelchairs and kids walking with IVs.

I swallow hard.

Ayla, Daniel and I walk down a long hallway. We pass under a sign that reads "Pediatric Cancer Ward" and past parents sitting on waiting chairs. We walk down a tight hallway. I see Maddie's Nana, no taller than five feet standing in a doorway. Nana smiles.

"Meh-ddie, your friends are here!" Maddie's Nana yells into her room in a thick Macedonian accent. She stands outside the room, greeting us with the best type of Grandma love.

"Hi, Nana." Each of us bend to hug her. I kiss her on the cheek.

"I'm sorry to hear about Maddie, Nana," I whisper. My voice cracks.

Maddie sits upright in a hospital bed. She is covered by a thin, blue sheet. She still has all her hair. The tan pigment is drawn from her skin and replaced with a grayish-white. She is hooked up to a heart monitor and an IV. Machines beep and blink red and green. The same hand sanitizer and latex smell has followed us into Maddie's hospital room. She smiles, showing the gap in her two front teeth. My favourite thing about her.

"Hey guys. I can't get up, sorry."

I look behind me and purse my lips together, trying not to start bawling. I remember what I told my sister: Let's try not to be sad around her.

Daniel's dark brown hair covers Maddie's face as he kisses her on the cheek. Ayla sits at the edge of the bed with the roses in her lap.

I walk over to her bed and hug her. I don't squeeze too hard. I don't know if she's fragile yet.

"Hey, Addy." She smiles. Her dirty blonde hair sits in French braid pigtails down her shoulders. I stroke the back of her head and smile.

"Hey, Madz. I got you something." I place the journal on her lap.

She picks it up with a pulse tracker on her index finger. Her wrist is covered in friendship bracelets. One reads "Fighter" in white beads. Another reads "BFF," with multicoloured plastic beads strung on blue and green thread.

"My writing professor said that writing for a couple minutes each day can help heal sickness." I play with the rip in my jeans. "I thought maybe when you're bored and don't have your Mom or Nana around then you would want to write your feelings or thoughts in here. Just an idea. Anything I can do to help you fight."

Maddie's eyes fill with tears. "Thank you, Addy." She smiles. "I'll try to write in it as much as I can. It might be a little difficult since I have jittery hands from chemo. Thank you so much."

I hug her again, noticing a large purple bruise on her chest, close to her throat.

~~~

July 22, 2015

Maddie and I sit on the porch of her historic house in Old Meadowvale Village. We shade ourselves from the heavy sun and sip on lemon water.

"Wait a second, I want to show you something." She leaps from the wicker couch and swings open the front door. Her tanned, muscular frame darts up the stairs.

Maddie hands me a familiar journal with quotes on the front. The cover frays around the edges and bends upwards. One quote is smudged from a water stain. The pile of clean lined pages inside the book now ripple on the bottom.

"I wanted to show you this." She sets the journal I gave her a year ago on my lap.

"You actually wrote in it?"

"Almost every day." She runs a manicured hand through her pixie-cut hair. "Even with my shaky fingers. The first three entries I wrote made me feel better about things, so I wrote in it almost every day after that. It kinda kept me company."

I open her journal to the first page.

All the Good Bits

I hunch over the desk huddled in the corner of my room. Houseplants hang above me and line the surface of my desk: succulents, cacti and a single fern. I scribble and flip the page, scribble and flip the page.

Big letters on sheets of my personalized stationary gather in a pile.

Love your granddaughter, Adelaide.

I fold the 6 sheets of paper horizontally three times so they will fit in one of those narrow envelopes, the kind that bills come in. The kind that people open without enthusiasm.

~~~

I check the mail every day, waiting for Grandpa to answer my letter. He is 83, so he might have trouble writing a whole letter. I haven't seen Grandpa Bruce since Christmas. It's now the end of January. Mom says his hearing is going, so the best way to learn more about him is through letters – our favourite way of communication.

I'm nineteen and I don't fully know my own Grandfather.

~~~

As I sprint back home from the mailbox, I step over the banks of snow as chunks fall and melt onto the path. Ice breaks off of mounds of snow that once trapped my car in the driveway. The pitter-patter of droplets collects in the rain gutters above me.

I swing open the front door of my house and kick my shoes off, not bothering to look down at my feet. I grasp Grandpa's letter in my hand and run up to my room. I close the door behind me and roll onto my soft white bed sheets. Levon, my gray cat jumps onto my bed with grace, barely making noise. The sun beams through my droplet-covered window – it's the first sunny day in almost three weeks.

I tear open the corner of the long envelope. I can tell this one is from Grandpa because of his handwriting in all capital letters. His handwriting is easier to read compared to Grandma Grace's eloquent, freehand cursive. She always tells me they practiced it in school during the Great Depression and that it's a shame we don't use it anymore.

Grandpa writes in a thin black pen, his capital words squish together. He still writes in a straight line.

January 28, 2014

Dear Adelaide,
I really loved the time we spent together in your growing years, the games we played, from making play-dough animals, to dress up, etc. Mostly before you started school, then your time was spent growing up and playing "growing up" games.

Grandparents really don't have much influence in the lives of their grandchildren. They love their children's children so much that they want to help them to understand and avoid life's problems and heartaches.

In your last letter, you asked me for advice from writer to writer, but I was never much of a writer – not books, not short stories, not essays, nothing that could be termed literary - Anything I knew about writing, I learned in high school. I wanted to be an artist – a "commercial artist," that was the term for an agency artist. I was successful, but if all failed as an artist, my plan B was writing.

What kind of writer do you want to be? There's fiction, non-fiction, journalism, the list goes on. But my job was writing and designing commercials, which led to writing radio commercials, which led to magazine articles about advertising, which led to writing industrial shows, executive speeches and so on and so on, and remember, this was all in the sixties, so things have certainly changed since then.

Oh, I could go on, but you're probably bored with all this palaver.

So Adelaide, as a grandparent who can't resist offering advice to a grandchild, read, read, read and write, write, write. Find your style or "voice." Find your favourite authors and imitate them- This happens in art, but in art, it's more obvious.

I was so happy to watch you graduate from high school – and launch into university. It's a big adventure - Try hard and enjoy all the good bits.

I love you,
Grampy OX

I fold up the papers and hold the letter to my chest. I look up at the ceiling and suppress my desire to cry. I told Grandpa I wanted to be a writer, and that I got into the Professional Writing and Communication program at UTM. Ever since then, him and Grandma send me their favourite books: Joseph Conrad's "Heart of Darkness', Jonas Jonasson's "100-Year-Old Man Who Climbed Out the Window and Disappeared", and Joy Kogawa's "The Rain Ascends".

I place the letter on my nightstand. I peer at a painting on my wall that has two pieces of paper coming out of a black typewriter. The papers read, "Late News" and in the bottom right corner of the picture is the name Bruce Walker. Grandpa gave this to me when I got accepted to the Professional Writing program.

I think about the kind of father he is to my mother, aunt and uncle. I think about how they always travelled with him from place to place as his job in advertising demanded he be in different places all at once. I can picture my mother, five years old with wispy red hair, latching on to his leg as he puffs smoke from a cigarette in a tailored suit. Him and Grandma have smoked since they were eighteen and haven't stopped. I know smoking kills. I also know they got lucky.

I wish I knew more about Bruce Walker. I wish school wasn't so stressful, and that I could play games with him like I did when I was little. I would still make play-dough animals with him.

I wish I spent less time playing "growing up" games, less time growing up so fast.

But I'm here. I'm nineteen, and although I may have grown up too fast, I know one thing to be true: that Grandpa was wrong. Grandparents do have an influence on the lives of their grandchildren. And because of the man who used to sit down in his art studio with five year old me and draw intricate cartoon pictures to match my made-up stories, I know I can be a writer.

Like Grandpa says, I better read, read, read, write, write, write, and enjoy all the good bits.

Just Like Your Mother

It's dark. The windows in the truck fog up. I adjust my knee. It digs into the door handle. I shift again. My knee unlocks all the doors.

"Sorry," I apologize.

My other knee lodges in the driver's seat armrest. I press my chest up against him to make sure my butt doesn't sound the horn. On the residential street we've parked on, people sleep in their houses. The neighbourhood rests. No one stirs.

He avoided parking under a streetlight. We don't want to get caught.

I look behind me. Mount Cypress towers over Victoria, British Columbia. The once cotton candy sky is now an infinite blanket of pitch-black. The lights in houses flicker as people turn them on and off. The arbutus trees sway in the warm summer wind.

His rough hands grab my face away from my gaze of the city and back to his mouth.

"Trying to soak up your last minutes in Victoria, *Sugar*?"

"Yes." I smile.

I run my fingers through his porcelain white hair. He tucks

my strawberry blonde hair behind my ear and plays with my fake diamond earring. My heart beats faster. I control my breathing.

What would I say if a cop caught us? I'm only nineteen. I could be his daughter.

He stops kissing me and sets his blue eyes on mine.

"God, you look just like your mother."

~~~

At Pho Mi 99 in Mississauga, I sip the remains of my honeydew bubble tea through a thick straw. Three cold tapioca pearls land on my tongue.

"Ad, I don't think there's any drink left. You've been at it for the past five minutes," Mum says and laughs. Wrinkles gather under her smiling eyes.

"There's one more tapioca pearl in there! What do you want me to do, stick my hand in the glass?"

"It'd be better than listening to you slurp."

"Fine. I'll give up."

The Vietnamese waiter walks toward our table with two bowls of steaming pho. He places the vegetarian in front of Mum and the wonton in front of me.

"Thank you," Mum and I say in unison. We never mean to say things at the same time, but it happens quite a bit.

Mum slurps her pho from the Chinese soupspoon. She catches herself slurping and snickers.

"Okay, now that we have our pho, tell me about your much needed trip of self-discovery."

I swallow hard. My fingers tap on the laminate wood table.

Mum's blue eyes stare up at me from her bowl. Raising her eyebrows, she waits for an answer.

"I have to tell you something," I confess. I rip the corners off of my white paper napkin.

Mum puts her bowl down. Clanging of porcelain bowls and silver cutlery mingle in the background. The same piano music loops overhead, the kind they play when a speech at the Oscars is too long. I bite the tip off my pinky nail.

"What is it? You're stressing me out. Did you get mugged? Are you pregnant?"

"Mum, what the fuck? No! Neither."

"Okay, then it can't be that bad." She adjusts her purple glasses.

"I made out with Steve. Like, a lot."

Mum pauses, laughs and tries not to spit out her mouthful of broth and Thai basil. She covers her mouth.

"Mum! Why are you laughing?"

She takes the paper napkin off of her lap and waves it over her face. Her mid-length auburn hair flies behind her. Her pale face flashes red.

Slowly, her red face goes back to white. She realizes I'm not kidding. She stops snickering.

"So you made out with Steve, huh?" She puts her napkin back on her lap and nods.

"Yes, I did. He just took such good care of me during my stay at his place. If I wasn't broke and actually stayed at a hotel all week, I would've been kinda lonely." I play with the ridges in the glass cup that once held the bubble tea. "He drove me around Victoria. I don't know. He's charming."

"He is charming, isn't he? That was one thing I loved about him back in high school. He used to drive me everywhere when I was in university too. I guess he hasn't changed much."

"So you're not mad?"

"Ad, why would I be mad? We're all human. We have needs. We have desires. Both of you are lonely."

"Mum!"

"Sorry," she apologizes. "Who cares? I obviously didn't marry him for a reason. He doesn't belong to me, so what's the big deal?"

I rub my sweaty palms on my black leggings.

"So you aren't mad I made out with your high school sweetheart?"

"Ad, come on! I'm fifty! That was many moons, and many men ago."

I take a deep breath and look down at my pho. The wontons bob in the soup as I stir it around. I bring the bowl to my mouth. It's room temperature. I look across the table. Mum's bony fingers wrap around the chipped bowl of pho.

"Well. That was less difficult than I thought," I say.

"Why would it be difficult? What would you want me to do, get mad at you? You're an adult. You can make your own decisions. That's your business now, not mine." Mum's thin frame leans in closer. "Now if I had this conversation with Grandma that would be another story. I didn't tell my mom anything, especially things like who I made out with. She would have kicked me out, but what would that have done? I'm not going to get mad at you, that wouldn't accomplish anything."

Mum pauses. "So, did you two do anything else?"

"Mum, gross!"

We go up to the till and pay. Mum rummages through her overflowing, worn leather wallet. She brings it up to her eyes and digs for coins. I stare into my wallet and see the green TransLink SkyTrain ticket I used to take me to the Vancouver airport. Behind it is a twenty-dollar bill. I look at Mum. Still rummaging for coins. The short elderly Vietnamese man behind the cash scowls and taps his long fingernails against the outdated register.

"Here." I hand him the twenty-dollar bill.

He grunts.

"Hey, thanks Ad."

"Of course, Mum." I smile.

~~~

I adjust my seatbelt. His truck drives away from our spot. We pass under streetlights. His hair glistens like the first snowfall under the orange sodium vapour lights that line the streets.

He looks at me and smirks. "Don't tell Mumma, okay *Sugar*? Our little secret."

I smile and nod. "Our little secret."

Appendix

January 18, 2016

The first time I ever saw him, he was standing outside Chako Korean BBQ Restaurant on a cold Thursday night in January. Through the frosty windshield of my car, I saw a tall, bulky man holding a pink gift bag and something the size of his arm wrapped in white paper. I adjusted my black see-through stockings and fiddled with the collar on my black and yellow striped turtleneck dress.

~~~

He first messaged me on Tinder back in December 2015. His pickup line was: "Hey Adelaide, are you my appendix? Because I don't know much about you but I have a feeling in my gut that I should take you out."

We talked on Tinder chat for a while. Then Tinder chat turned into texting, then texting turned into long phone conversations.

The first picture I ever sent him was during one of my last closing shifts at Starbucks while I rolled and dragged the industrial garbage bin out to the disposal. My nose was rosy because of the cold. He thought that was cute.

It had been nearly four years since I was called cute.

Slowly and all at once he broke my loneliest four-year streak.

When I asked what he did for a living, he told me he worked in the film industry.

"I love your name, I actually work on Adelaide Street East. How do you pronounce it?"

"Ahh-duh-layd"

"Beautiful."

~~~

I look at my blue-green eyes in the rearview mirror of my white Hyundai Accent. The silvery-gold sparkles in the inner corner of my eyes reflect off of the fluorescent green Chako sign. I blend my blush in with my fingertips. *Too much.* I do a teeth check.

I take a deep breath and remember what my friend Lyndsay told me, "Who cares what he looks like. You guys have been talking every night for almost a month so at this point, do looks really matter?"

I reach a pointed black boot out of my car door. My heart races. I pull my striped dress further down my butt.

Modesty, Ad, modesty.

I remember what Dad said, "Don't give it all away on the first date."

As I walk toward the front doors of Chako, I finally see him up close. The Chako sign reflects off his shiny brown curls. The curls gather in the middle, the sides shaved to a fade.

"Hey, Jack?" I inch toward him, purse on my shoulder, clammy hands behind my back.

He turns around. Even with heels on, he towers over me. He's 6'4. I'm 5'4 ½. He holds a bouquet of a dozen red roses like a swaddled newborn. Strong arms hand them to me with the same carefulness and close attention as a day-old child.

"Here, I got these for you." His deep voice is shaky. The wrapping paper on the bouquet crinkles as I retrieve it. His lips part to reveal a gentle smile. Brown eyes and long lashes hide behind Buddy Holly glasses.

"Oh, and this, too. When we were on the phone, you told me you ran out of M&M's and Nibs in your candy stash, so I got you some more."

I try to stop my smile, trying not to mess up my lipstick.

"Thank you." I bring the roses up to my face and inhale, one rose now less fragrant than the rest. I peek inside the pink bag of goodies. I stand on my tiptoes and wrap my arms around his neck, and smell him for the first time. As I bury my head into his shoulder, cold and cologne take up all the air in my nose.

"Here, let's put these in my car."

~~~

"I didn't expect your voice to be this deep," I say, huddling in my covers and holding my iPhone up to my ear.

"Yeah, a lot of people say I have a radio voice, but I think they're full of it."

Definitely not full of it.

"So, why did you decide to download Tinder?"

"Uhm, good question," I say. "My sister and mother got tired of watching me read, write and see the same friends every weekend. My Mum even told me a few weeks ago that if I don't start looking for a man, I'm going to die alone. Just me and my books.

"So Lexi downloaded the app for me, chose my best pictures, and showed me how to swipe left if a guy is ugly. I hated the whole concept of it. It was superficial and I didn't really take it seriously. But I guess I got Tinder because the whole meeting someone organically thing wasn't working out for me." I pause. "What about you?"

"Same thing, I guess. People told me to get it because they thought I was trapped in this monotonous routine. I guess I was. You're the only girl on here that hasn't tried to hook up with me. I hate hookups."

"You're the only guy who has greeted me by name and not 'Sexy,' or 'Babe.' "

"That's how it should be."

~~~

After Korean BBQ, we went over to Bubble Tease. We drank an artificial honeydew slush with extra tapioca in my car while 102.1 The Edge hushed on the radio.

"It's weird that you covered your mouth while eating at dinner. Do you normally eat like that?"

I laugh, "Oh, jeez, you caught that? I was trying to be polite!"

"What the fuck? Polite? Who eats like that?" He laughs.

I shoot him a scowl and sip my green slushy drink. "I didn't want you to think I was a slob," I say with a mouthful of tapioca.

I hear his laugh for the fifth time. I want to hear his laugh always. "Turn Your Love" by Half Moon Run plays on the radio. I twist the dial to increase the volume. With a single finger, I tuck my barbeque-scented hair behind my ear. I turn my head and Jack's cold lips press against mine. His beard brushes my made-up cheeks. We kiss to the rhythm of the song, with artificial honeydew on his tongue.

The windows fog.

~~~

February 14, 2017

Jack and I sit cross-legged around a white box on my cream quilted bed sheets. A dozen red roses stand straight in Grandma's old vase on my nightstand.

"I meant to give this to you for our one year, but, you know, I got carried away."

"It's alright, babe." My eyes meet his. We smile.

I open the box to reveal a white album with "Jack and Adelaide" painted in black calligraphy on the cover. Pink, hand painted flowers circle the lover's names. Thin painted twigs, and dark purple lavender hang off the branches. I open the book, turning the pages slowly, studying it as if I were looking through old pictures. Because I was.

The first page reads, "The start of a new story…" It's our first Tinder conversation.

I rest the book on my legs and put my head in my hands.

Jack rubs my back, "Come on, babe." He laughs. "You haven't even made it through the first page and you're already crying?"

I laugh. "Okay, okay, I'm good."

"So I might have re-downloaded Tinder to get our first conversation back."

"No way…" I sniffle.

I flip through each page, trying not to get my fingerprints on any of the photos.

Collections of pictures join little marker drawings of objects: a dozen roses, inside jokes, and ballet slippers from when we first saw The Nutcracker, cover the pages.

Collections of pictures from our days spent in Toronto

Appendix

are displayed in rows. Photos from our first vacation together in Vancouver, British Columbia stack on top of each other: Lynn Canyon, the Sea Wall, Granville Island, and pictures of me posing in front of trees and by the ocean. I flip through more pictures. Old, but still so new.

~~~

Ever since I was little, I didn't think I was going to get married. I was at my best when I spent time alone in my room. No one to bug me, no one I have to talk to. I let the world exist around me as I spent my time floating in a bubble, not unlike the Good Witch's Bubble from *The Wizard of Oz*. I could stay there and not come out.

I don't like to say I met Jack on Tinder, but that's modern love, I guess. I feel like I knew him in a past life; maybe we were two undiscovered planets. I think this is our first life being lovers.

He changed everything. I had an image in my head as to what my life was going to look like. I didn't see a lover. I was my *own* lover. I thought it would just end in divorce, so why even try? I saw myself travelling, not being tied down. I thought it would be wasted energy trying to find someone who I liked more than characters in novels, or being alone. But when I met him, he showed me I was looking for happiness in all the wrong places, if I was looking for it at all.

~~~

I flip to the final page of the scrapbook. The last page of the reads my favourite quote by my favourite poet, Sylvia Plath:

"I took a deep breath and listened to the old brag of my heart.

> I am,
> I am,
> I am."

To my loving girlfriend, here's to all the years ahead of us.
> You are,
> You are,
> You are.

The Poet

Incomplete

I might just be half of something
Not knowing which half I am
But as long as
I am living
And you are breathing
You will always be
The rest of me

Half Moon

Some say
Binaries are most useful when challenged
And maybe when we break it's never into clean halves
So let's not break
Let's stay huddled under the sheets
Pretend the bed is a boat and we are stranded on a vast ocean
Empty
But not lonely
So let's not break
Let's keep being the binaries
You can be one half
And I can be the other
So when our hands meet your fingers can slide into mine like a zipper.
Some say binaries are most useful when challenged
But I don't need to challenge you because we lie together on this worn out mattress in the middle of the ocean
And the last thing I want to do is question your intents
Let's not make this tense
Why would I Challenge you because
You make it so easy for me to love you
So let's lay in the middle of the Atlantic looking at the stars and darling maybe we can let the Sharks rock another boat
Because we won't need help doing that tonight
Let's not break into halves
Let's become whole
Like the orb of night
That shuts out the dark
And wait until the sea
Rocks us to sleep

Almost Afterlife

If I died tonight
I think I would like to come back as your bed sheets
Keeping you warm when you're most vulnerable
And making it hard to leave me in the morning
Or maybe I would be your glasses
I get to help you see things all day
And if you take me off, you're helpless
But if you just so happen to wear your contacts all day, maybe
I would want to be a fluff on your sweater
You will never notice me there but boy am I holding on.
But wait,
One day you'll throw the sweater in the dryer and I'll be gone
So for now
If I died tonight
I would wait for you on a park bench in our favourite park
And wait until we could join all of the other dead lovers
in the stars

In the Skin of the Universe

On nights like these
She stays awake to keep him company
When you can't sleep, my darling,
I will stay awake and paint the entire universe on the back of your hand
So you don't feel so alone when I have to leave you again
So you have the whole galaxy to keep you company
The galaxy will run its fingers through your hair
its long nails leave traces that hurt
but feel just like mine
rough, but gentle
She stays awake to keep him company
When you walk in at 10:30 p.m. holding a bag of chips and a club soda, I'll spring out of bed and feed you
Rummaging through the bag for the wish chips
The ones that cower over themselves
You open your mouth,
"Make a wish," I say, yawning.
She stays awake to keep him company
I dust eyelashes off your cheek
catching one with my index finger
I hold it in front of you
It lays on my fingerprint
A tiny piece of you
Sitting atop a microscopic part of me
I hold the eyelash up to your face
"Make a wish," I say, yawning.
I roll over and look at the clock
11:11
"Make a wish," I say, yawning.

She stays awake to keep him company
to teach him that rain will wash away everything
but only if you leave your umbrella closed
only if you let the rain erase the things that haunt you at night

She lays beside him to keep him company
We leave the window open
And let the rain pour in

12:37 A.M.

Last night I cried because I love you so much
But I don't know why
They were both happy
And sad tears

8,705

I will do all I can
To make time for the things you love
For the things we love
I will hold your hand for the eight thousand seven hundredth and second time
And hold it like a child holds a balloon
Darling don't fly away from me
When I'm not around
Grasp your own hand in the other
Close your eyes
And pretend it's me
Pretend we are linking pinkies for the eight thousand seven hundredth and third time
When I'm not around
Do not miss me
I won't call you every night
But I will try and find a little more good in me
To give to you
So when we are together
We can make time
For the things we love
Eight thousand
Seven hundred
And four times

Peace be with you

Every man
Whose laid an unwanted finger on this
body that I call home
has had a name from the Bible.
And I pray for their sake
that they one day realize that a woman's
body
and blood
is sacred;
is theirs.

I've never been a churchgoer
but I've sinned enough to know
that it is the woman who
is God
and the man
who is the visitor
the worshipper
sometimes the lover
but
never
allowed
to outstep his welcome
or let my body disintegrate on his tongue

The man may not
drink my blood from a chalice.

Last October

I got rid of the perfume I wore when I knew you
Because I didn't want to smell like those days I spent chasing you
A never-ending path to destruction

I got rid of the perfume I wore when I knew you
Because unlike your scent,
Mine still lingers
On the words you could never say back.

Sorry Song

Dear Mother,
I'm sorry I left you when I was sixteen,
Nothing but a sick teen
Your house was two sizes too small
and like our stomachs, your wallet was two sizes too empty.
I wish I didn't eat meat back then
An extra twenty dollars a month you didn't have.
I wish I could have cut that bill in half.
Until one day I did
I thought I was doing you a favour
Handed you the false promise that, "I'll be back later,"
But I wasn't.
Once I moved out, I was gone for good
Left you and Lexi with hearts emptier than all of our stomachs.
I kicked myself out.
Thought I was doing you a favour
Maybe making your burden lighter
One less mouth to feed
One less person using all your water
Your oldest daughter
Always looking out for you.
So Mum,
I'm sorry that after five years your wounds have not healed,
only scabbed over
and over
and over again.
I'm sorry your bank balance didn't reflect the amount of
work
I thought I was doing you a favour

Doing Dad a favour.
You see, he seemed so lonely
in a new house,
Echoing with the empty sounds of no woman to love it
Echoing with the sounds of, "Well, it's only fair, right? Mum has one daughter and Dad has the other!"
My Mother.
I'm sorry for making you feel unloved.
When Dad went to bed, I would wait to hear his steady snores like a heartbeat
I would sneak out of the house and at sixteen,
I would drive his BMW to the nearest convenience store for a slushie; the kind that leaves your tongue black and blue.
I would pay fast,
Leave fast
Just in case dad woke up
But there was just one thing – in order to arrive at the convenience store,
I have to pass your house
It's on the way there.
I slow down in a car two sizes too big for me
At 12:53 a.m.
I can see the light in your bathroom through the window of your leased townhouse.
It takes everything not to run in
and kiss you good morning.

Sessions

Something about telling all of my most
suppressed emotions
to someone I don't even know
makes me feel
clean.
Something about sitting in front of a human being
Who has problems just like I do
Makes me feel like
I should be the one asking,
"How has this week been for you?"
But I can't tell you
how this week has been for me
because I can't help but wonder
if my therapist
needs therapy, too.

The Wasteland

I'll wait until May
After the cruelest month
Because everyone gardens then
But what if I want flowers in the middle of the winter
When nothing seems to be growing?
It is said that April showers bring may flowers
But what if I don't want to wait that long?
I guess I will just plant kisses like seeds
on your body
And wait for them to grow.
But my love,
Don't pick them
Because these little darlings are as delicate as our love
And seem to be surviving in the snow
My not so dainty flower- can't you see you leave gardens every time you walk away?

Playground Games

Just when I tried to forget you
Forget us
I felt the seeds you planted in my ribcage
Growing like wild vines.
The vines then turned into flowers that sprouted just below my collarbones.
Now I spend my days plucking each petal off what used to be nothing but a seed
I pluck
And pluck
And pluck
But I still can't quite figure out
Whether you love me
Or not

Bombyx mori

If I loved you
I would have let you go
I would have let you leave my side on a dull winter night
And watched as you got smaller and smaller as you headed down the street
The only thing leading the way are the endless sets of streetlights
But if I never see you again, I would have to learn to be okay.
We could always meet in the stars
Or maybe we would somehow run into each other in another life
You could be a silk moth
Or a new planet
And I could be the lightbulb
Or that one star that keeps you company as you figure out what being a planet entails
But if you choose to stay on land
I won't turn on the lights
I would read your address my the moon
And I'll call your name like we're playing hide and seek
I'll repeat it
And repeat it
And repeat it
Hopefully you hear me
Just in case it's the last thing you hear
Hopefully you hear me
Just know
I did my best to find you
My silk moth
My new planet

Paper Cranes

They say if you love someone let them go
So I will fold you into a thousand
tiny paper cranes
fold each corner tight so you won't come undone
and watch as the wind
sweeps you up
and lets you go once you reach your
favourite constellation.

They say if you love someone let them go.
I guess I'll see you in the stars

The art of following

If I chase your echoes down long hallways
Will you be waiting for me behind the door
Ready to catch my breath?

The First and Last Snowfall

I stare out the window
Flecks of white blur my vision
Your silhouette is stark against the bright white snow
I can no longer see your features
I forget what you smell like
Just a silhouette
Just a vignette

I draw the curtain back in its rightful position
Dusty, opaque

Howling circles beat at the window
Only glass between us

The light that never goes out

I close my eyes and count to ten
It's dark and like everyone's eyesight is past midnight mine isn't the greatest
I get on all fours and search for you as if I lost a contact lens
I feel you
Your cozy body waiting for me
As I sail alone around the room
Spinning
I think to myself
What am I looking for?
Your hands grab me and I fall into you like a child whose father's just come home from work
Hug you for too long without even letting you put the briefcase down
It is no wonder you are in this dark room
Just when I thought I was alone I remembered you once told me
That if we cannot find the light,
We will always make our own.

"When the tongues of flames are in-folded
into the crowned knot of fire,
and the fire and the rose are one."

- T.S. Eliot, *The Little Gidding*

Acknowledgements

    Thank you to my family who has always been in my corner – Dad, thank you for smothering me with generosity in its many forms, and for your unwaivering, unconditional love and support. Because of you, my dreams are now a reality. Mom, you have always nurtured and encouraged my love for reading and writing from such a young age. And Lexi. My little sister and best friend, thank you for never leaving me alone, and always listening to my stories – written or not. We have been through so much as a family, but I know we are stronger for it. And to my Nanna and Nannu who have always made everything easier on me. May roses always grow from your garden.

    And to Jack, my dearest boyfriend. Thank you for your unceasing patience. Thank you for breathing life and creativity into my cover page and inspiring the last story of this book. Thank you for staying up late with me all those nights we spent mercilessly typesetting and perfecting this book. You are selfless in so many ways.

    The poems in this book would not have bloomed if it weren't for all of my friends at poetry circle, and my number one fan Brent Wood. Without Professor Wood my love for poetry would still be hiding someplace dark and gloomy. You served me my passion on a sliver platter and I am eternally grateful.

Thank you to Ms. Kappl, my first best friend. You made the roughest years of my childhood more bearable and always gave me a safe space to be myself. I would not be where I am today if it weren't for you.

Thanks to all of my friends who have always accepted me just the way I am – Cat, Arthur, Hutch, Alexa, Maddie, and Ayla. You have taught me so much about myself, and the world around me.

And lastly, thank you to Guy Allen and John Currie for believing in me. You always pushed me to write the not-so-frilly stories and have proven to me that you can make a life for yourself through writing. Thank you from the bottom of my heart.

About the Author

Adelaide Clare Attard is a recent graduate from University of Toronto Mississauga with a double major in English and Professional Writing and Communications. A women's rights activist and aspiring vegetarian, Adelaide lives a cruelty-free lifestyle. You can find her walking up and down the aisles of Whole Foods or sipping a matcha green tea latte at a local coffee shop, enjoying Canadian literature and the works of her favourite poet, Sylvia Plath. Adelaide currently resides in Mississauga, Ontario with her Maltese Yorkie, Ollie. She hopes to be a journalist, editor or poet, some day.

Made in the USA
Columbia, SC
27 December 2017